D1717154

How Do I

Manage My Social Media?

Sarah Eason and
Ruth Bennett

CHERITON

CHILDREN'S BOOKS

Please visit our website, www.cheritonchildrensbooks.com to see more of our
high-quality books.

First Edition

Published in 2022 by **Cheriton Children's Books**
PO Box 7258, Bridgnorth WV16 9ET, UK

© 2022 Cheriton Children's Books

Authors: Sarah Eason and Ruth Bennett
Designer: Paul Myerscough
Editor: Jennifer Sanderson
Picture Researcher: Rachel Blount
Proofreader: Wendy Scavuzzo

Picture credits: Cover: Shutterstock/Liza888. Inside: p1: Shutterstock/insta_photos;
p4: Shutterstock/MPH Photos; p5: Shutterstock/carballo; p6: Shutterstock/
baranq; p7: Shutterstock/StudioSmart; p8: Shutterstock/Margot Petrowski; p9:
Shutterstock/Africa Studio; p10: Shutterstock/Iakov Filimonov; p11: Shutterstock/
Kseniia Perminova; p12: Shutterstock/Syda Productions; p13: Shutterstock/Mavo;
p14: Shutterstock/Flamingo Images; p15: Shutterstock/pathdoc; p16: Shutterstock/
Seasontime; p17: Shutterstock/Roman Samborskyi; p18: Shutterstock/Elena Elisseeva;
p19: Shutterstock/Rawpixel.com; p20: Shutterstock/paulaphoto; p21: Shutterstock/
Iakov Filimonov; p22: Shutterstock/myboys.me; p23: Shutterstock/insta_photos;
p24: Shutterstock/Donna Ellen Coleman; p25: Shutterstock/Syda Productions; p26:
Shutterstock/diignat; p27: Shutterstock/Rawpixel.com; p28: Shutterstock/fizkes; p29:
Shutterstock/Yuriy Golub.

Printed in the United States of America

Contents

Help! How Do I Manage My Social Media?

#Help! What's social media? That's something you'd never say, right?! Yup, if there is one thing kids know about today, it's social media. From watching funny videos and looking at cute pictures to chatting online with friends, social media has opened up a whole world of fun. But how can you control your online world, and why do you need to? Let's find out!

Social Media—What's So Great?

Social media has forever changed the way we **communicate** with other people. These are just some of the things it helps us do:

- Keep in touch with our friends.
- Make new friends—all over the world.
- Join online clubs.
- Get involved with charities.
- Keep up with the latest trends.

People love sharing their world with others, but it's important to learn how to do that safely.

In recent years, social media has been more important than ever, particularly during lockdowns.

Not So Fun?

Although social media is mostly great, it can have a **negative** effect on us. From reading upsetting posts to feeling that our lives aren't as great as everyone else's, social media can make us feel bad. That is why it is important to know how to control your social media. Managing your social media is all about getting the most out of it. It's about learning how to use it to stay **connected** with the people you want to connect with. It's about knowing how to use those connections to improve your life and the lives of others. And it's about understanding how to protect yourself from dangers online.

#Help!

Where Do I Start?

When it comes to managing your social media, the best place to start is by involving your parents or guardians. You may think that sounds boring, but it can help you **navigate** what can be a difficult world, and keep you safe.

Chapter One

Help! How Do I Use Social Media?

#SoMuchSocialMedia! It's everywhere! So many great sites, so many people to talk to, and so much to say! This amazing network can connect us to thousands, if not millions, of people. It allows us to share our thoughts with others, and find out what they think, too. Awesome! But hold on—before we start sharing, we need to learn how to do it well.

Hey, World, Here I Am!

So there is a big World Wide Web out there. How do you want it to see you? That may sound like a funny question, but when you **socialize** online, you are introducing yourself to the world. That's why it is worth taking time to set up your social media. Before you dive into use this amazing

You Can Hack It!

It's tempting to create a profile that makes you sound like a superstar! You could say that you are a child billionaire or that your dad is a rock star. But this could backfire on you if people find out the truth. What do you think are the benefits of being honest?

tool, you need to learn how to feature yourself on it. That means how you want to present yourself to the cyberworld, and how you want it to **perceive** you.

It's All About Me!

The first step when starting to use a social media site is to create a profile. This is information that tells people who you are. It can tell people all kinds of things about you, such as what hobbies you have, what you like and dislike, and who you follow online. It's a little like meeting someone for the first time and finding out all about them. So what do you have to say about yourself?

#Hack: When setting up a profile, avoid using silly names. They could come back to haunt you! For example, would you like a future employer to learn that you were once called "Fluffy Bear"?!

How Do I Make a Profile? #Help!

Think about who you really are and try to show that in your profile. Here's how to do this:

• Tell people what your interests are, such as what hobbies and sports you enjoy.
• List your likes and dislikes.
• Take a look at the profiles of people that are similar to you, and that you like. Are there any features they use that you could use, too?

How Do I Chat Online?

Taking part in conversations online gets your profile noticed, so, let's get talking! There are a lot of different ways of using social media to talk to other people. For example, you can post status updates about what you are doing, and **comment** on other people's posts. You can also link to other sites, such as blogs. Ready to chat? Let's learn how.

You can write a blog anywhere, and it's a great way to get thoughts out into the world.

Be a Blogger

A blog is an awesome way of sharing your ideas. And if you link your writing to what is happening in your local area or something featured on the news, people are likely to take an interest. Blogs tell others about your skills and knowledge, too—and that's a great way to impress someone! Remember, though, it's always a good idea to tell your parents or guardians what you're posting before you put it online.

How Do Kids Start Blogs?

Sites such as Fanschool are specifically designed for kids who want to blog. Why not check it out?

What Do You Think?

Most social networking websites allow people to comment when something is posted. This can often be the beginning of a conversation with others, and it may even lead you to new interests and ideas. Remember that comments can be viewed by others, so always be polite and respectful. Be sure that you use sites designed for young people, and always let your parents know what you're doing online.

Always Ask If It's OK

If you want to share a photo or a blog that shows or mentions another person, remember to ask for their **permission** before you post it. This is because the person in the photo or the blogger might not want you to include them in your post. Everyone's online profile is personal, so be careful not to upset people by doing something that they might not like.

You Can Hack It!

Can you think of a situation in which someone might be upset if you posted a photo of them without their permission?

How Do I Start a New Chat?

Some people are really scared by the idea of beginning a conversation online. If that is how you feel, don't worry—it's natural. Many people are nervous about beginning a chat. The good news is that starting a conversation is something that you can easily practice. And the more you practice, the easier it will become. So, let's talk about talking...

Friends First

It's easy to start a new conversation with some of your friends who are online, too. If you have a new interest, try telling them about it. Once you are confident that you can speak to your friends, you can start to speak to other people that you don't already know. #CheckYouOutChatty!

Like It? Talk About It!

Whether you are talking to people online or in person, people like to talk to others with similar interests. So if you want to start an online chat, think about posting about something that you like and are interested in. It could be your pet, the music that you like, or even where you went on vacation. And when others join the chat, you'll probably find that you have a lot to talk about. You can learn a lot from other people, too. For example, if you post about food you like, others might share their recipes, too.

If you are nervous about starting a conversation online, begin with a group chat with your friends.

What's Going On?

People are always interested in what is going on in the world around them. If you have seen something interesting in the local or national news, you could post about it. It could be a serious story, such as **climate change**. It could be something funny, such as a silly video someone posted online. Whatever the **topic**, invite others to comment and to add what they have to say.

How Do I Start a Post? #Help!

Here are some great tips for starting a post that will get people talking:

• Start with a question. For example, you could say, "Do you love dogs or cats the best?"
• Share a funny joke or story.
• Include a funny video or picture—but always make sure it is not **offensive**.

#Hack: If you love cooking, share photos of the amazing recipes that you have made.

Chapter Two
Help! Why Should I Be Careful?

#WishIHadn'tGoneOnline! Have you ever posted something and then **regretted** it? Perhaps you've joined in a conversation that has turned ugly. Maybe you've said something unkind, or someone said something unkind to you. Have you viewed something online that has upset you? While social media can be great, it has its downside, too. People may say things online that they wouldn't say in person, and people can get hurt as a result. It's important to be aware of the downsides of Internet socializing so you can learn how to protect yourself online.

Cyberbullying—It's Cruel

We've all heard about cyberbullies. These are people who post mean things about other people to bully them online. They may **mock** the way they look, or **criticize** the way they talk. They may tell lies about others. They may joke about someone's race, **gender**, or **social background**. Cyberbullies hide behind a computer or cell phone screen. They use it as a shield behind which they can say the meanest things without **consequence**.

Every year, thousands of children become victims of cyberbullying.

Remember, one day you will probably apply for a job. Keep that in mind when you post online.

Out There Forever

When you post a photo or a video online, you may think you can delete it and no one will be able to find it again. However, the Internet doesn't work like that. It is impossible to completely erase, or remove, something from the Internet. A photo or video uploaded years ago can be found and used in the future by people if they look hard enough for it. For example, when you apply for a job 10 years in the future, a potential employer could find a photo that you posted when you were just 14 or 15 years old.

#Help!

How Do I Protect Myself Online?

When you use your social media, always follow these key rules:

- Report cyberbullies. Tell your parents, guardians, teachers, or friends if you think someone is cyberbullying you.
- Never post photos, videos, and even comments that you think you may later regret. Never upload anything that could damage your **reputation** now or in the future. If in doubt, don't do it.
- Do not visit adult websites. They may contain advertising that is **inappropriate** for you or adult **content** that can be upsetting. Don't allow friends to encourage you to look at those sites, either. Tell your parents, guardians, and teachers if you are at all upset about anything you have seen.
- Ask your parents or guardians to help you learn how to block and report anything you find upsetting.

What Should I Share?

Using social media is a great way to chat with others and share news about what you're doing. But it is important to first think carefully about what you want to share, how you share it, and who you want to share it with. There are ways you can manage your social media to prevent you from sharing everything with everyone, and upsetting others, too.

Uh, Oh! Wish I Hadn't Done That...

Social media sites all have privacy settings. These are really useful as a way of controlling who can see what you post online. If your posts are can be seen by everyone, make sure you don't post anything that will have a negative impact on the way people see you. You might be happy to share a photo of yourself when you were three years old with your best friend, but do you really want the world to see it? Thought not!

You Can Hack It!

Why do you think people might share things online that they don't share in person? What are the dangers of doing that?

Stop! Don't Send!

Talking online uses only written communication. The good news? This means you can prepare what you want to say in your own time, without any pressure. The bad news? Once you have posted something, it is out there for the world to see. So always think about how the things you post will affect others. This means that you shouldn't be negative about them or write anything you wouldn't say in person.

Remember to think about how people might react to your posts before you put them online.

#Help!

Why Shouldn't I Copy?

Avoid copying something that another person wrote and pretending that it is your idea or **opinion**. That is called plagiarism, and no one should do it. #Don'tCopy!

What Are the Dangers?

The sad truth is that there are some adults who go online to contact young people and children. These individuals often pretend to be a young person or a child themselves. They create an online "character" who talks like a child, to fool children into believing that they are talking to a friend and someone their own age.

What Is Grooming?

When an adult makes friends with a child online with the intention of **manipulating** them, it is called grooming. The grooming often starts in online group chats, but then moves to private chats. The adult may **persuade** the child that they only want to be friends with them. They may pretend to share the same interests and hobbies. They may use the same games and apps, to persuade children that they are just like them. However, these adults are a threat.

One of the biggest dangers of social media is online grooming.

It can sometimes feel like everyone's life online is better than yours.

Feeling Bad

Social media can make people feel bad about themselves. For example, some people seem to have the perfect lives in their posts. They have the best clothes, the best homes, and the best vacations. It seems that nothing ever goes wrong for them. That isn't real, even though it can seem true. Adults often unfairly **compare** themselves to other people online, and it's the same with children. It's important to remember that no one's life is perfect and that everyone has problems, even if it seems like they don't.

#Help!

How Do I Stay Safe?

There is a lot that children can do to protect themselves from the dangers of people who use social media wrongly. When using social media, you should always do the following:

- Avoid putting the name of your school or your address on your profile.
- Avoid sharing personal details in posts, such as where you go to school, where you live, or your telephone number.
- Use a strong password on your profile. This is a word that others will not easily be able to find or guess.
- Switch off any location services. This will stop others from finding out where you are.
- Never make friends with strangers. If you do not know exactly who the person is in real life, don't friend them online.
- If someone talks to you online and then asks for personal information about you, never give it.

Chapter Three
Help! What Is Social Networking?

#NetworkNeedToKnow! Do you know what social networking is? Nope? Well, the fact is, you probably already network without even realizing that you're doing it! Networking is a huge part of social media. But, what is it and why is it useful in every area of your life?

Let's Link Up!

Networking is all about forming connections with other people. You network every day when you use social media. For example, when you say hi to your friends online, you are networking. You also network when you talk face to face with people.

Hey, Here I Am!

Networking tells people all about you. This is important because if people know about you and what you are good at, it helps you find opportunities. For example, perhaps you are a great photographer. If the school newspaper needs some photos of an event, you would be the perfect person to take them. But first, the people who run the

#Hack: Crazy about horses? Networking will connect you with other people who love horses, too.

Social networking connects you with a lot of different people, all at the same time.

newspaper need to know who you are! That's where social networking comes in. When you network, opportunities to get involved in exciting activities are more likely to come your way.

Networking—What's in It for Me?

For some people, networking will be just for making new friends. Other people will want to learn more about a new hobby, or make sure they find out about interesting things that are happening in their area. Every person will have different networking goals. You will get the most out of your networking experience if you decide what your goals are before you start. A popular networking goal is learning from people who have more experience than you. For example, if you love baseball, you could learn more about it from more experienced players.

#Help!

How Do I Start Networking?

To start your social network, follow these simple steps:

- *Prepare*: Think about what your interests are.
- *Read*: Find websites that match your interests.
- *Write*: Think about how to describe yourself and your interests. You could post that description as a profile.
- **Interact**: Go to the websites you've discovered and talk to people. Find out about them and tell them about yourself!

How Do I Use Networking?

Networking is all about **exchange**. Every person in the world has special skills and ideas. When you connect with other people and share ideas with them, it can help you in every part of your life. That includes connecting with other people to work on projects, such as homework. As the saying goes, two heads are better than one!

Problem Busting

A great way of developing ideas is sharing them with others. Have you ever tried to figure out something on your own and gotten stuck? By sharing the problem with someone else, you are more likely to find the solution. So the next time you are struggling with a homework problem or where to buy a new pet, tap into your social network.

In the Know

Networking conversations can be easier if you already know a little bit about your topic. For example, if you need help with a difficult project, do some **research** before involving your network. Carrying out some research in advance will help you ask the right questions. But what if you want to join a conversation that has already been started, but you know little

You Can Hack It!

Can you think of a project or problem that your social network might be able to help with?

about the topic? Again, try to do a little research first. That way, when you join the conversation, you will feel you have something to add and are less likely to say something silly!

#Help!

How Do I Ask My Network for Help?

Here's what to do if you have a problem or a project that you would like to ask your network to help with:

- Give your post a heading, such as History Homework, Help Needed.
- Write your question or questions clearly.
- Read back through your questions before posting, to make sure that they make sense.
- When you post your request, always thank your network for any help they may give you.

#Hack: Background reading can help you learn about something you want to talk about.

How Else Can I Use My Network?

So, we've learned that your network is pretty neat. It links you up with a ton of people. It allows you to make new friends and talk to old ones. You can ask people in your network for help and advice. You can offer your own advice and knowledge, too. And there's more...

What's Up?

Networking is a fantastic way to find out what's going on and learn about the latest trends. New trends often become popular by word of mouth or by "going viral." If you have a large network, you are sure to hear about them! #I'mSoOnTrend!

Helping Out

A good social network is made up of people who know you and like you. They should be eager to help you whenever they can, just as you will help them. A network of people will support you when you are trying to achieve something, whether it is a sponsored run or a science competition. People in your network will also be happy to share their network with you. They might not be able to help you achieve your goals, but maybe they know someone who can, and would be willing to introduce you to that person.

If you need help with a science project, why not ask your social network?

Even a five-minute conversation can help you reconnect with your network.

Keeping Connected

You'll get the most out of your social media if you keep up with what your network is doing. If someone writes a post that interests you, make contact with them and find out more. Keep up to date with your online network to stay connected.

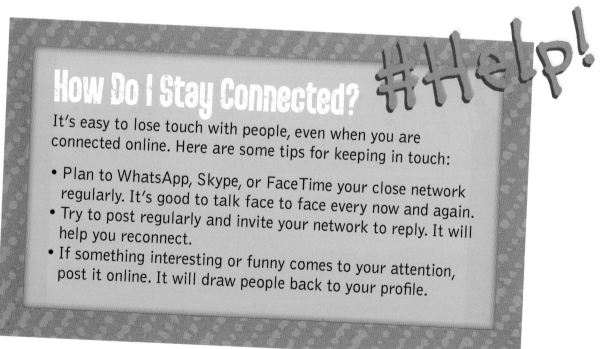

How Do I Stay Connected? #Help!

It's easy to lose touch with people, even when you are connected online. Here are some tips for keeping in touch:

- Plan to WhatsApp, Skype, or FaceTime your close network regularly. It's good to talk face to face every now and again.
- Try to post regularly and invite your network to reply. It will help you reconnect.
- If something interesting or funny comes to your attention, post it online. It will draw people back to your profile.

How Do I Network Face to Face?

Networking online is an amazing tool, but networking face to face is just as important. While speaking through a screen is **convenient**, there are times that we need, or want, to talk to people in person. #SayWhat?! OK, that may sound like something your mom or dad would say, but talking in person is something we all need to do. It's good for us, because having in-person contact with other people makes us feel good. So how can we learn to network well out there in the real world?

Say It with a Smile

When you meet someone new, remember to smile! If you smile at people, they are likely to smile back. A friendly face is far more **approachable** than a face with a miserable or bored expression! Smiling is a signal that you are willing to talk, and it's the best way to start a conversation. Once you have given a friendly smile, beginning to chat is much easier.

Keep It Simple

When you are talking to people about your interests, remember that they might have little or no knowledge of the subject. Keep your explanations simple, rather than overwhelming the other person with facts. Showing **enthusiasm** helps, too, because people are then more likely to listen to what you are saying.

#Hack: If you smile when you first meet people, it will help them relax, too.

Talking on-screen is useful and can save time, but it is also good to spend time with people face to face.

How Do I Talk to People?

Learning how to ask questions in person is an important networking skill. When you are talking to people, remember these tips:

- Most people respond well if you show an interest in them. If you ask their opinions and listen to what they say, they will feel that you care about their ideas.
- It's important to pay attention to what people tell you, and to respond by asking further questions as a way of finding out more.
- If you are shy, it can be tempting to speak quietly or to mumble when talking to someone new. However, you should always try to speak clearly, so people can understand what you're saying.

How Do I Keep On Networking?

The ways that you use your network will change as you grow up, but the connections that you make can last a lifetime. Through your network, you may find you make friends that will become friends for life. Networking never stops. And, as you gain confidence, you'll start networking without even knowing it—#NetworkKnowItAll!

Nail It with Networking

As an adult, networking will help you with work. A **professional** network is made up of other people working in the same area. It helps you find out about developments, trends, and job opportunities. Your network will allow you to find opportunities, take on new roles, and work with people who have interests and goals similar to yours.

A group of professional dancers may belong to the same network.

As you grow up and enter the workplace, your network may center on other professionals.

Networking—What's Next?

The Internet is still young. As time passes, the way that we use it is likely to change. Social networking is already a huge part of our lives. It's changed the way we study, work, and interact with other people. Today, the Internet is a major part of how we network. Keeping up to date with new developments in social media and technology will be vital to successful networking in the future.

#Help!

How Do I Keep on Track?

As your network grows, you might find it difficult to keep track of. Think about what your networking goals are, and organize your time so you can achieve them.

Help! How Do I Stay in Control?

#SussedMySocialMedia! OK, so you know how to chat, what to post, and when to walk away if you don't like what you see or read. Feel like a social media pro? Want to be the king or queen of chat? Great, but before you dive back in, just remember to...

#Hack: Remember to only post things that make you and others feel good.

Keep It Friendly

Don't forget, your online profile includes all of the comments you have posted, and all of the things you have linked to. That means someone can look at what you have written and shared, and use that information to learn about you. If you have said or shared something mean, people may think you are a mean person. It's important to always be kind, just as you would be when speaking to someone face to face.

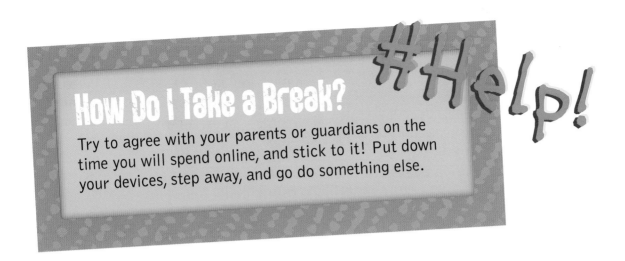

How Do I Take a Break? #Help!

Try to agree with your parents or guardians on the time you will spend online, and stick to it! Put down your devices, step away, and go do something else.

Take Time Out

Using social media can be fun, but too much time spent online isn't good for us. Sitting in front of a screen for hours on end isn't healthy. It can stop us from sleeping well if we are online at night. It also stops us from moving around and exercising. It stops us from communicating with people face to face, too. It's important to take breaks from social media. Remember, there's a whole world out there, and it's not inside a screen!

When Things Change

As you grow older, managing your social media will change again. As you start to use social media for more grown-up activities, you will likely have more sites to navigate and more people to chat with. But as long as you keep in mind the things you have learned in this book, you can control your social media and it won't control you! #HappyDays!

And finally— #NotJustForKids! Learning to manage your social media now will set you up for a long life of happy sharing.

Glossary

approachable seemingly friendly and easy to talk to

climate change a change in the average temperature and weather patterns in a place over a long period of time

comment speak or write about something that someone else has said or done

communicate exchange information or opinions with other people

compare note differences between things

connected joined to

consequence a negative result or effect of an action or situation

content the information included in something

convenient useful and easy

criticize point out the flaws or find fault with something or someone

enthusiasm strong excitement and interest in a subject or an activity, and an eagerness to be involved in it

exchange giving or taking of one thing in return for another

gender a person's sex, such as whether they are male or female

inappropriate out of place or not suitable

interact communicate and react to other people

manipulating controlling or influencing in a sly or dishonest way

mock make fun of or imitate

navigate find one's way through something

negative bad or damaging

offensive rude or upsetting

opinion a person's view about something that can't be proven with facts

perceive become aware of something specific

permission approval to do something

persuade try to make someone do or think something

professional relating to work that needs special training

regretted felt bad about

reputation how someone is viewed or thought of by other people

research find out about something

social background the environment in which someone has grown up, including where they live, their education, and how wealthy their family is

socialize spend time with other people for enjoyment

topic the subject or main idea of something such as a speech

Find Out More

Books

Entrepreneur Media Staff. *Entrepreneur Kids: All About Social Media*. Entrepreneur Press, 2021.

Greve, Meg. *Social Media and the Internet*. Rourke Educational Media, 2018.

Raum, Elizabeth. *Social Media Savvy: Facts and Figures About Selfies, Smartphones, and Standing Out*. Capstone Press, 2018.

Websites

For a simple and safe blogging site, try Fanschool:
https://go.fan.school/kidblog

YourSphere is a global social networking site where kids can connect and interact:
https://yoursphere.webs.com

Instagram offers a fast and fun way to share photos with friends:
www.instagram.com

At Kidzworld, you'll find a safe social networking site with plenty of features, such as quizzes, chat rooms, games, homework help, and information on health, careers, style, travel, and much more:
www.kidzworld.com

Publisher's note to educators and parents:

All the websites featured above have been carefully reviewed to ensure that they are suitable for students. However, many websites change often, and we cannot guarantee that a site's future contents will continue to meet our high standards of educational value. Please be advised that students should be closely monitored whenever they access the Internet.

Index

About the Authors

Sarah Eason has written a wide variety of children's information books. Ruth Bennett has written many informative and entertaining books for children. In writing this book, both have learned a lot about social media and how to manage it.